Early Literacy - A Seasonal Approach

by
Helen K. Raczuk
&
Marilyn P. Smith

U-Otter-Read-It™
Helping Teachers
Help Children

1st printing by
2 otters celebrating their
3rd year, and their
4th publication

U-Otter-Read-It © 1999

All rights reserved. Except as noted,
no part of this publication
may be reproduced or transmitted
in any form or by any means -
graphic, electronic, mechanical
or by telecommunications
without the prior written permission
of the publisher. -
or, in the case of photocopying
or other reprographic copying,
a license from
CANCOPY (Canadian Copyright Licensing Agency),
One Yonge, St., Suite 1900
Toronto, Ontario
M5E 1E5

Purchase of this book entitles the BUYER to reproduce designated pages, for classroom and instructional purposes only. In other words - if that nice teacher down the hall wants a copy of your book, tell her to buy her own! The families who depend on Helen and Marilyn, thank you from the bottom of their hearts, for buying this copy, and respecting copyright.

Canadian Cataloguing in Publication Data

Raczuk, Helen K., 1952-
Early literacy

Includes bibliographical references.
ISBN 0-9681074-3-5

U Language arts (Preschool) 2. Reading (Preschool) I. Smith, Marilyn P., 1953- II. Title.
LB1140.5.L3R32 1999   372.6   C99-910701-1

Published by
U-Otter-Read-It
11 Miller Place, Spruce Grove, Alberta
Canada
T7X 2N1
http://www.uotter.com

Printed in Canada

Early Literacy - A Seasonal Approach

Acknowledgements

We gratefully acknowledge, first of all - the authors and illustrators, who created the words and pictures which have inspired us to create this book. Making selections was difficult, and many titles were not included - simply due to size constraints of the final publication. However, we are otterly grateful for this collection of stories and pictures, which has so much potential to delight, inspire, and greatly enrich early literacy experiences.

We also acknowledge the support and encouragement of the following people, without whom, our efforts would be seriously lacking in energy and quality!
- Stephen Smith & Ron Chenger - for expertise in layout and computer work
- Lorraine Anderson - Audrey's Bookstore, Edmonton, for suggesting titles
- John Gregory - J Gregory & Associates - for web design, and for believing in otters
- our family and friends - who continue to support, and encourage our efforts

Dedication

This book is dedicated to our Canadian weather!
The ever changing seasons in our country,
inspire incredible creativity
as evidenced by the tremendous
body of literature,
music, art
and designs
which celebrate
and honour
the blessings of the seasons.

A deo de quo omniae benedictae exflugent

Helen & Marilyn

Table of Contents

A Few Words About This Book 7
Strategic Teaching Ideas 11
Strategic Teaching Planner 14
Great books 16

Autumn 17

The Pumpkin Blanket, Teaching Ideas 18
Pumpkins, MB 21
My Blanket, RTS 23
Tools for School, MB 24
Fall is Around Us, RTS 26
My First Day at School, MB 28
Leaves in Autumn, RTS 30
Back to School, MB 31
Summer's Done, RTS 33
Wheels on the Bus, MB 34
Rainbow Zoo, MB 36
Hippos on a Fence, RTS 38

Winter 41

Sadie and the Snowman, Teaching Ideas 42
A Frosty Friend, MB 45
Dreaming of Winter, RTS 47
The Storm, RTS 49
Winter Storms, MB 50
Everything Went Wrong, RTS 52
Do You Have a Minute, Santa? RTS 54
Friends Forever, RTS 56

Spring 57

The Garden, Teaching Ideas 58
Planting the Garden, RTS 60
Spring Is, pattern book 61
Sheepish Barbershop, RTS 62
Drip, Drop, Rain, RTS 64
Love Comes, RTS 65
Hoe Down for Spring, RTS 66
Here's to Mothers, RTS 68
My Mom, MB 69
Recipe for A Dad, RTS 71

Summer 73

Take Me Out to the Ballgame, Teaching Ideas ..74
A Fan's Request, RTS 76
A "Berry" Good Skipping Rhyme 77
Any Kind of Bugs, RTS 78
Bibliography 79

- *MB - Mini-Book
- *RTS - Readers Theatre Script

Early Literacy - A Seasonal Approach

Early Literacy - A Seasonal Approach

You are warmly welcomed to this, our 4th **U-Otter-Read-It** publication. <u>Early Literacy - A Seasonal Approach</u>, was written to help teachers organize those great picture books in a practical, learner-supportive system, so that they could be useful throughout the entire year.

It is our firm belief, that the enjoyment of quality literature should be the basis for sound and effective, early literacy instruction.

Titles have been organized into seasonal themes, to complement the seasonal approach many primary educators use to organize the instructional year. Sub-topic, within each season have also been identified, highlighting such themes as: family and friends, colours and numbers, weather, and special holidays.

It is our hope that this organization will assist the teacher in making selections from the many titles available for children, to use in the development and extension of early literacy skills.

Guiding early readers through collaborative and individual activities towards independence requires observation, and constant analysis and assessment. This is the challenge all literacy teachers face, and it is our hope that the models we have provided will serve to support and guide educators to extend and further develop their own classroom instructional approaches.

Four titles have been selected, one for each season, and have been expanded to address strategic early literacy instruction. Activities are designed for *Before, During and After* interaction with the book. In conjunction with these titles, consider enriching reading opportunities for your children, by providing them with other reading materials. We strongly encourage you to obtain multiple copies of several titles, where possible. Keeping several copies on hand for easy access, while stories are being featured, is a strong incentive for a young reader to read with partners and on his own. It is through revisiting stories that children develop as readers. While we have suggested titles for specific seasons, please keep in mind that this does not mean, that some titles cannot be enjoyed all year long!!

Included in this book, are several original scripts. Readers Theatre is a highly motivating activity which offers children the opportunity to develop reading skills in a collaborative,

A Few Words about This Book

quality literature forms the foundation for solid instruction

seasonal organization supports planning for the instructional year

Strategic Teaching

strategic early literacy instruction models provided

Readers Theatre Scripts

supportive setting. As scripts are read together, children are exposed to a variety of reading strategies. Fluency and expression improves through continued practice, and more importantly, confidence grows as the children begin to view themselves as *readers*.

planning for readers theatre is an on-going process, based on growth evident in student's skill and confidence

When planning readers theatre in your classroom, consider grouping children to effectively address and accommodate individual needs. Struggling readers can be paired with more independent readers to familiarize them with the text, and support their own emerging strategies. As improvements become evident, more challenging parts may be assigned. More importantly, however, view this as an opportunity to group struggling readers together, to address specific skills when common problems and needs arise. This may be viewed as a critical teaching-moment, where mini-lessons can be taught, and skills, required for success in reading, can be reinforced.

readers theatre supports balanced early literacy programs

As you prepare to present a text, determine
- challenging vocabulary
- natural rhymes and rhythm of the text
- meaning or message of the selection.

model desired reading behaviours

Guide the children through the script, supporting them by modeling desired behaviours. Read expressively, interpreting characters using a variety of different voices. Read expressively, using pauses and tempo for dramatic emphasis. Encourage students to experiment with their own reading style, seeking the BEST way to present the script. Children will rise to the challenge to become excellent storytellers and ultimately, confident, independent readers.

Mini-Books

Mini-books are a great way to follow-up a shared-reading experience. They provide opportunities for children to explore and practice concepts, vocabulary, and patterns experienced in the book. They also give children the opportunity to add their own interpretations of the text with their own illustrations, or words. To assemble the mini-books, photocopy the reproducible pages, fold into four, then slip the second page inside – like a greeting card.

mini-books as assessment tools

Teachers may use these mini-books as tools for assessing the ongoing progress of each student, and observing individual literacy development.

We have purposely chosen to make these books relatively

Early Literacy - A Seasonal Approach

generic in that one mini-book may be used as a follow-up to several titles within a shared theme. Where possible, draw children's attention to similarities between the stories read, and the mini-book formats.

Two types of mini-books are included in *Early Literacy - A Seasonal Approach*.

page 24, 50

• *Tools for School* is an example of a ready-made text, where the story line is provided for the children. The simple repetitive pattern allows children to focus on early reading skills such as tracking, directionality and the use of picture clues.

• *Winter Storms* is a sample of a mini-book which uses a cloze framework for students to create their own story based upon their personal understanding and response to text.

The following teaching strategies are beneficial when working with mini-books:
• Preview the text and illustrations with the children to make connections with the literature you have shared in the classroom.

· Encourage children to explore the text in a variety of ways.
    · count the number of words on a page
    · locate specific words in the text
    · find words starting with specific sounds or letters
    · listen for rhyming words
    · identify unusual looking, or familiar words

• create a cloze from the text by omitting either words or letters depending upon the needs of the children. Read the selection together and ask students to reread it and fill in the spaces. Verbalizing the words and listening carefully are keys to success. Some children may need to refer to the original text for assistance. This activity helps develop an awareness of visual cues and develop phonemic awareness.

• Make copies of the mini-books available so that students may benefit from reading the book in a small group or with a partner. In the same way students benefit from having access to a classroom library, easy access to the mini books provides several opportunities to revisit text, and ultimately become independent readers.

• Mini-books, and readers theatre, are tools which complement any home-reading program. Consider creating a duo-tang or

mini-books focus on specific instructional needs

cloze activities promote understanding of semantic and syntactic systems

mini-books should be treated as an instructional and reinforcing opportunity

initial experiences with reading highlight early literacy skills*
· directionality,
· tracking,
· letter/sound knowledge
· rhyme

cloze activities reinforce phonemic awareness

it is through revisiting text that students develop as independent readers

establishing and maintaining communication with parents strengthens early literacy programs

U-Otter-Read-It © 1999

Early Literacy - A Seasonal Approach

modeling provides support for emerging writers, while stimulating and inspiring confident writers.

Insert an envelope at the back for mini-books. The children can also consider including a page for comments from the parents, and you, to update each other on achievements and successes.

• When students are creating their own mini-books, do an example with the class to model the possibilities for vocabulary and language patterns. Discuss and list useful words, especially emphasizing colourful vocabulary derived from the stories you have read together. Through discussion and consistent modeling, children build a supportive foundation, and develop resources to enrich their personal writing.

• Once children have created their own mini-books, provide several opportunities for them to share their creations with peers, school buddies, other adults as well as their families.

We have created activities which have been designed to be adapted and serve as models for you when developing your own ideas and mini-books. Each script or mini-book can be modified to meet student needs by varying the amount of teacher direction. For example, even the simplest script will challenge an independent reader, if asked to create a new script modeling the existing pattern. The teacher may model the process first, before turning it over to an individual or small group to develop on their own.Carefully consider the literature used in your classroom to determine how it might support the needs, extend the skills, and enrich the interests and opportunities for your students. Keep in mind that sometimes a good story should be allowed to remain, simply, a good story, in order to stir the imagination and excite the potential of young readers and writers.

Early Literacy - A Seasonal Approach

Before, During & After Reading
Ideas for Strategic Teaching

Reading Strategies	Activities	Classroom Example

Provide & Develop Background Information in Preparation for Reading

Before, During

• discuss ideas and concepts related to the story
• read other literature meaningfully connected to the story
• encourage reflection and sharing of personal experiences that are relevant to the text "Today we are going to read a story about a winter storm. Have any of you been out in a storm?"
• model personal connection to the themes and concepts key to the story.
• share information about the author. Show a picture, if possible.

• Bring in a treasure box, with items related to the story. For example, a picture of a snowstorm would be appropriate to introduce ' *Belle's Journey*', along with a toy horse, mittens, a rope, candle, and other objects relatedto the story and to winter storms.

Preview the Text

Before

• scan the text looking for key words, text features
• encourage early readers to tell what they know from the text
• point out unusual features, such as interesting text, or unfamiliar words

• Ask: "Here's an interesting word. What do you know about this word? "Expect responses such as: 'it starts with the same letter as my name ....it has 7 letters in it. "

Set Purpose for Reading

Before, During

• seek specific information "When we are done reading, see if you can tell why the story is called……"
• compare to previous stories…."See if this story reminds you of another we have read.
• guide children to create images … • "Imagine yourself riding on a horse, in the middle of a very strong, cold blizzard. Your face stings, and you can't feel your fingers. What do you see? How do you feel?"
• notice descriptive vocabulary or unknown words

Provide students with an 'anticipation' page. Give a few 'facts' related to the story, and ask children whether they agree or disagree with the facts. Following the story, review the facts, asking again, whether they agree or disagree. If answers are changed, ask 'how do you know'. Encourage revisiting text to check answers.

U-Otter-Read-It © 1999

11

Early Literacy - A Seasonal Approach

Ask Questions & Make Predictions

Before, During, After

• W's & H's - who, what, when, where, why and how

• make connections to characters, events, setting, problem, solution

• use the title as a basis for questions to make predictions

• use leads as models,
  • *"I think, I predict, I wonder…"*

• support questions and predictions with reasons
  • *" I think…because…."*

• use graphic organizers for recording predictions and tracking events and storyline
  • *what really happened in the text"*

Use diagrams, storyboards or other visual aids, to help children see the sequence of the story. It is essential that the story be re-read several times, providing the opportunity to hear, see, and add more details with each reading.

Independent writers might enjoy the opportunity to keep a journal, recording their response to characters and events in the story. Emergent writers may use more drawings to record their responses, with as many words and ideas as they are comfortable to write. Children might write "If I were _____, I would _____". or "I felt _____ when _____ because ____."

Visualizing

Before, During, After

• visualize story events, characters, and setting
• picture descriptive passages as they are read aloud
• use flannel boards or story boards to gather details about setting
• predict what the setting or characters look like based on known information

Encourage children to draw pictures of the characters, or settings in the story. If necessary, provide a framework for their drawing, asking: 'what do we need to have in the picture where Goldilocks comes into the cabin?" Responses should include: table, chairs, bowls of porridge, - perhaps a door leading to another room. These pre-discussions assist children who may have missed details the first time, and need additional guidance when deciding what to draw.

U-Otter-Read-It © 1999

12

Early Literacy - A Seasonal Approach

Monitoring Understanding

During, After

• on-going process-predicting, confirming, clarifying meaning as the story is read
• Build a repertoire of **fix-up strategies**
  • Read on
  • Re-read
  • Think-aloud
  • Think about what is happening in the story
  • Look for parts of the word that seem familiar
  • Sound out the word
  • Ask for help

• Model strategies during story times, chart reading, and direct teaching using 'talk aloud'

• discuss the plot and the characters

Work with individuals or small groups, and ask questions requiring each student to articulate the process being used. For example :¨
• does that word make sense?
• read ahead, and see if that word really fits there.
• what is another word that would make sense in that spot?
• does that word start with the same sound as this one

Recall Analyze Organize Summarize Information

Before, During After

• apply knowledge of story characters and plot to oral interpretation
• respond to the story with personal reactions, opinions
• create a new story based on the pattern or theme of the old one or find other stories in the same genre
• Build early literacy skills by revisiting the text several times. Provide activities, which require readers to go back for specific details.

Seat children in a small circle, and give the first child a ball of string. This ball is made of strings of various lengths, knotted together. The child begins to retell the story, unwinding the string as they talk. When a knot is reached, they pass the ball on to the next child, who continues - even if in mid sentence.

U-Otter-Read-It © 1999

Early Literacy - A Seasonal Approach

Strategic Teaching . . .
Before, During & After Reading Ideas
to Use With
Title _____

Reading Strategies		Activities
Provide & Develop Background Information in Preparation for Reading	Before, During	
Preview the Text	Before	
Set Purpose for Reading	Before, During	
Ask Questions & Make Predictions	Before, During, After	

U-Otter-Read-It © 1999

Early Literacy - A Seasonal Approach

Visualizing	**Before, During After**	
Monitoring Understanding	**During, After**	
· **Recall** · **Analyze** · **Organize** · **Summary Information**	**Before, During After**	

Guide Questions

- What would happen if
- Do you know
- Do you see
- How does it start
- How does it end
- Can you find _____ that sounds like / looks like
- This story makes me feel / reminds me
- I wonder if
- I remember when
- This is just like

- The funniest / saddest / scariest part was when
- I'm thinking of a word that sound like / looks like ....
- These words rhyme with
- Find a word that starts like your name / ends like your name
- The picture makes me think that
- Were you right
- How did you know

U-Otter-Read-It © 1999

Great Titles to Use All Year Long

Author	Title	Themes
Andrews, Jan	The Auction	change
Harris, Dorothy Joan	Four Seasons for Toby	all seasons
Hughes, Shirley	Wheels	birthdays
Heidbreder, Robert	Eenie Meenie Manitoba	poetry
London, Jonathan	I see the Moon, the Moon sees me	
Molnar, Gwen	Animal Rap and Far Out Fables	poetry
Shaw, Nancy	Sheep in a Shop	birthdays

My Otter Favourites

Early Literacy - A Seasonal Approach

Activities listed on this page are applicable to stories grouped in particular theme areas. Consider partnering the feature story with one or two others listed from the same category, then use the reproducibles for introductory or follow-up activities.

Great books for Autumn	Activities	Page
Security blankets		
The Pumpkin Blanket	*Teaching Activities*	18
Franklin's Blanket		
Ira Sleeps Over	*Pumpkins* - Mini-book	21
Selina and the Bear Paw Quilt		
Something from Nothing	*My Blanket* - Readers Theatre Script	23
The Quilt Story		
The Whispering Cloth		
Letters and Numbers		
A to Z	*Leaves in Autumn-*	30
A Mountain Alphabet	Readers Theatre Script	
Doggies	*Summer's Done -*	33
My Arctic 1, 2, 3	Readers Theatre Script	
My Little Sister Ate One Hare	*The Rainbow Zoo* - Mini-book	36
My Love For You	*Hippos on a Fence -*	38
One Gray Mouse	Readers Theatre Script	
Ten Little Rabbits		
The Wildlife 1 2 3 Counting Book		
Going to School		
Franklin Goes to School	*Tools for School* - Mini-book	24
It's the First Day of School		
Oliver Pig at School	*My First Day at School* - Mini-book	28
The Wheels on the Bus	*Back to School* - Mini-book	31
	The Wheels on the Bus - Mini-book	34
Weather		
November Boots	*Fall is Around Us -*	26
Simon and the Wind	Readers Theatre Script	
Waters		
Colours		
Brown Bear, Brown Bear, What do you See?	*The Rainbow Zoo* - Mini-book	36
Mouse Paint		
My Crayons Talk		
Those Green Things		
Autumn Holidays		
Jillian Jiggs to the Rescue	*Pumpkins* - Mini-book	21
Trick or Treat, Little Critter		

U-Otter-Read-It © 1999

Early Literacy - A Seasonal Approach

The Pumpkin Blanket
by D. Turney Zagwyn

Before Reading

children identify with personal experiences to predict events in the story

Clee enjoyed playing pretend with her blanket. Before reading the story, tell the children that they will need to listen for all the imaginative ways that she used her blanket. Invite the children to share ways that they have used blankets for pretend games. For example - they may have turned their blanket into a tent, or a batman cape, or a magic flying carpet.

- foreshadowing events in the story
- relating stories with familiar themes
- relating to personal experiences and events

Children might know about Linus (Charlie Brown) and his special blanket. Bring in a video, or cartoon book, featuring Linus. He is an expert on playing pretend with a blanket

During Reading

Read the story. After, list all the different things that Clee did. For example, she used it as
- a tent
- a skirt
- a dance partner

identifying specific details to listen for, prior to reading the story, sets purpose

Ask children to bring in special blankets or toys that they have had for a long time - or that hold special meaning. Why do children have a special blanket? Why do children have a favourite teddy bear? Perhaps they may share stories of having the blanket as a reminder of someone they love, who is no longer with them.

Invite children to tell about the history of that item. Questions to ask might include:
- How long have you had _____
- Where did you get it? or
- Who gave it to you?
- What makes it special?
- Describe your _____
- What does it feel like? look like? How big is it? What is it made out of?

Take pictures of each child with their special toy or blanket. These photos and stories will be used later.

After Reading

Refer to the lists the children made about their pretend games, and their descriptions about their blanket. (or teddy bear) Together, write the following blanket story.

    My blanket is _____(size)
    and it _____ (looks like)
    My blanket feels _____ (how)
    when I _____ (do what, feel how?)
    My blanket can be a _____ or it can
    be a _____.
    I love my blanket!

drawing information from text to develop and expand thoughts expressively

When children are comfortable with the sentence frames, invite them to write their own blanket story either independently or with a partner. Add their photo to their story - or display the story with their photo. Consider creating a class book of blanket stories.

providing young writers with a frame supports insecure writers by connecting personal experiences with events found in the story

Read one of the following stories to the children, then compare the following elements with the *'Pumpkin Blanket'*. Use a Venn-diagram, or a chart*, as a way of visually comparing elements such as: character, problem, setting, events.
- *Franklin's Blanket,* by Paulette Bougeois
- *Ira Sleeps Over,* by Bernard Waber
- *Selina and the BearPaw Quilt,* by Barbara Smucker
- *Something from Nothing,* by Phoebe Gilman
- *The Quilt Story,* by Tony Johnston
- *The Whispering Cloth,* by Pegi Deitz Shea

grouping stories and poems with similar themes helps children recognize common threads explored by writers through a variety of literary genres

After the children have read other stories, they may develop a comparison chart*, similar to the following. Consider having the children draw pictures as well as writing words, to show the similarities and differences between the stories. It may be helpful to organize the material on a bulletin board or pocket chart, allowing easy manipulation of information. Pictures might also be added, depending on needs of the students.

Charts are a good technique for visually organizing ideas and words. Children can easily see similarities and differences. Information can be quickly sorted, manipulated and located.

Consider using pocket charts as a quick way to organize and sort information.

	Pumpkin Blanket	**Selina and the Bear Paw Quilt**
Main Character	Clee	Selina
Blanket description	• 12 patches • colourful	• patches • colourful • made by grandmother
What happens to the blanket?	• it is taken apart to be used as a cover for the pumpkins	• it is given to Selina to take to their new home - where it is treasured as a special reminder of the family that stayed behind
How does the character feel about the blanket?	• quite attached, as it has been used ever since Clee was a baby	• very sentimental, and much beloved, as it was made by grandmother. Holding the quilt reminds Selina how much she loves her grandmother - it's almost like hugging her grandmother.

Read the script, *'My Blanket'*, with the children. Encourage them to identify feelings and sentiments found in the script, which may be similar to their own. Consider adding and changing ideas, to relate more closely to those of the children within the class.

page 23

Reproduce and distribute copies of the mini-book *'Pumpkins'*, to the children. Encourage them to practice reading with a partner, and to take the mini-book home to share with parents. Be sure to have an adult listener sign the child's book, to indicate that they have shared their reading with someone, and to serve as encouragement to read more.

page 21

To accompany *Blanket* stories

(page 6, inverted)

to greet all the kids
on Halloween night.

(page 1, inverted)

Pumpkins in gardens,

U-Otter Hear Me Read!

I have read this book to:

Words to practice	Let's Rhyme!
in	light
and	night
they	sight
all	tight
the	bright
to	fright

U-Otter-Read-It © 1999 May be reproduced for classroom use

Pumpkins

4

Pumpkins to carve,

3

pumpkins to water and weed while they grow.

5

pumpkins to light,

2

pumpkins in rows,

To accompany *Blanket* stories

My Blanket*

by Marilyn Smith

Reader 4   A blanket to cuddle in the dark night,

Reader 2   when winter winds whistle

and snowflakes take flight.

Reader 1   A blanket to snuggle next to my cheek,

Reader 3   when I've had a bad day, or worse -

ALL   a bad week!

Reader 2   A blanket to carry,

Reader 3   a blanket to keep,

Reader 1   a blanket to huggle[+] when I can't sleep.

Reader 4   It's only a square of cottony cloth,

with rows of wee teddy bears

dancing across.

Reader 3   I imagine they're singing soft lullabies,

while I drift off to sleep

and close my green eyes.

Reader 1   It's my blanket to treasure,

though tattered and worn.

Reader 4   It's been mine forever -

ALL   since the day I was born.

*this script is dedicated to Kathryn Smith - for sharing her blanket with me… M.P.S.
[+]Huggle - a hug and a snuggle

9

and don't forget
your smile!

L

Remember to bring
your notebooks.

U-Otter Hear Me Read!

I have read this book to:

Words to practice	Let's Rhyme!
to	take
your	make
and	cake
take	bake
	lake
	rake
	shake
	flake
	wake

U-Otter-Read-It © 1999 May be reproduced for classroom use

Tools for School

To accompany *School Stories*

Tools- continued

U-Otter-Read-It © 1999

3

Remember to bring
your crayons.

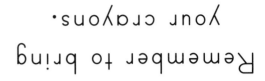

4

Remember to bring
your scissors.

Remember to bring
your pencils.

2

Remember to bring
your running shoes

5

To accompany *Fall Weather* stories

Fall is Around Us

by Marilyn Smith

ALL	Fall is -
Reader 1	[pencil]s and paper,
Reader 2	[pencil]s and glue,
Reader 3	playing at recess,
Reader 4	and learning in [school].
ALL	Fall is -
Reader 2	[pumpkin]s, zucchini,
Reader 4	green beans and such,
Reader 3	[corn] on the cob,
Reader 1	and [apple]s to munch.
ALL	Fall is -
Reader 4	cool winds blowing,
Reader 3	[leaves] all a'flutter,
Reader 2	[tree] branches blazing,
Reader 1	skies filled with colour.

Fall is Around Us - To accompany *Fall Weather* stories

ALL	Fall is -
Reader 3	geese flying south,
Reader 1	and ⬭ matches,
Reader 2	while 🐻's fill up
Reader 4	in berry patches.

ALL	Fall is -
Reader 2	sweaters and 🧥s,
Reader 3	red rosy cheeks,

Reader 4	cool evening walks,
Reader 1	and fields of wheat.
ALL	Fall is -
Readers 2 & 3	floating and drifting
Readers 1 & 4	all around us.
	without a doubt,
	fall is
ALL	upon us.

To accompany *School* stories

9

Can I go to school tomorrow?

I went for recess.

1

My drawing of my teacher

I met my teacher.

 U-Otter Hear Me Read!

I have read this book to:

Words to practice	Draw some things that rhyme with sat.
I sat a my to go	

U-Otter-Read-It © 1999 May be reproduced for classroom use

7

My First Day at School

I coloured a picture.

4

I sat in MY desk.

3

First Day - continued

I printed my name
like this –

I heard a story.

5

2

To accompany Fall Weather stories

Leaves in Autumn
by Marilyn Smith and Helen Raczuk

Reader 3   1 🍁, 2 leaves
Reader 4   red and orange and brown.

Reader 1   3 leaves, **4** leaves
Reader 2   tumbling, drifting d o w n.

Reader 3   **5** leaves, 6 leaves
Reader 1   yellow, green and red.

Reader 4   7 leaves, **8** leaves
Reader 2   falling on my head!

Reader 1   9 leaves, **10** leaves
Reader 3   toss them all around.

Reader 2   Crunching leaves, crackling leaves
Reader 4   🧹 them in a mound.

Reader 3   Hundreds of leaves, thousands of leaves
Reader 2   d a n c i n g with the breeze.

Reader 4   Millions of leaves, billions of leaves!
Reader 1   falling from the trees.

9

1

_____
_____
_____
_____
_____
_____
_____
_____
_____
_____

To accompay *School* stories

This is me.

Today's Activities

U-Otter
Hear Me Read!

I have read this book to:

By _____
Grade _____

U-Otter-Read-It © 1999 May be reproduced for classroom use

7

Back to School - continued

4

3

_____
_____
_____
_____
_____
_____
_____
_____
_____
_____

This is my teacher.

This year I hope

What You Should Know About Me

My drawing of the best part of the day.

_____
_____
_____
_____
_____
_____
_____
_____

5

2

To accompany *Letter and Number* stories

Summer's Done

by Marilyn Smith

ALL	One, 1
Reader 1	Summer's done.
ALL	2, two
Reader 4	What shall we do?
ALL	Three, 3
Reader 3	Jump in the leaves.
ALL	4, four
Reader 2	Pile some more.
ALL	Five, 5,
Reader 3	Let's take a dive!
ALL	6, six
Reader 4	Colours to mix.
ALL	Seven, 7
Reader 1	Geese are calling.
ALL	8, eight
Reader 3	Birds migrate.
ALL	Nine, 9
Reader 2	Never-mind.
ALL	10, ten
Reader 4	School again.

To accompany School stories

(page 6)

all the way   to

(page 1)

go round and round,

The 🛞 s   on the

U-Otter Hear Me Read!

I have read this book to:

Words to practice	Look in the story. Can you find words that start with the same sound as:
the on go to way school	  

U-Otter-Read-It © 1999 May be reproduced for classroom use

The
Wheels
On The
Bus

Wheels- continued

4

goes 'ssh, ssh, ssh.'

on the

The

3

go yak, yak, yak.

on the

The

5

The

on the

goes honk, honk, honk.

2

The

on the

go swish, swish, swish.

To accompany School stories

(Page 6)

Come and see the animals at the Rainbow Zoo.

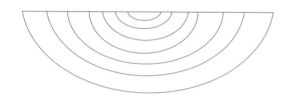

(Page 1)

9 white butterflies

10 purple hippos

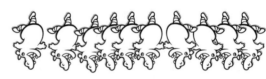

U-Otter Hear Me Read!

I have read this book to:

_____

Print the number that matches each word.

six	____	nine	____
five	____	ten	____
seven	____	four	____
eight	____	one	____
two	____	three	____

U-Otter-Read-It © 1999 May be reproduced for classroom use

The Rainbow Zoo

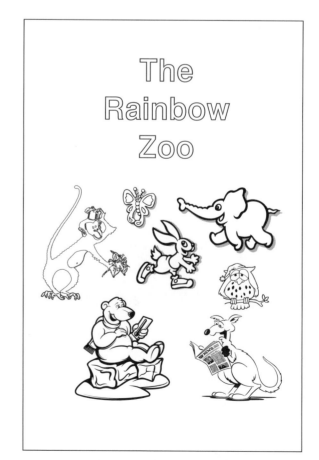

Rainbow Zoo- continued

3

5 green monkeys

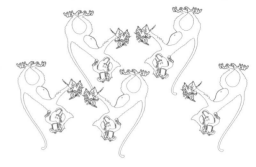

6 brown elephants

4

3 blue bears

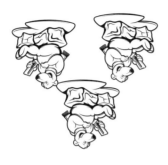

4 orange lions

2 black snakes

1 grey kangaroo

5

8 yellow rabbits

7 red owls

2

To accompany *Letters and Numbers* stories

Hippos On a Fence

by Helen K. Raczuk

Group 1	10 tremendous hippos twirling on a 🪵 -
Group 3	one lost his 👟, that wouldn't do,
ALL	so that left 9.
Group 2	Nine nimble hippos galloping on a fence -
Group 4	one stubbed his toe, he had to go,
ALL	so that left 8.
Group 3	Eight eager 🦛s skipping on a fence -
Group 2	one had to STOP, and off did flop
ALL	so that left 7!
Group 1	Seven SILLY hippos hopping on a 🪵 -
Group 4	one started to giggle, the fence did wiggle,
ALL	so that left 6.
Group 2	Six serious hippos dancing on a 🪵 -
Group 1	one stopped to bow, he fell - somehow!
ALL	So that left 5.

U-Otter-Read-It © 1999
may be copied for classroom use only

Hippos on a Fence - To accompany *Letters and Numbers* stories

Group 3	Five **FEARLESS** hippos frolicking on a 🚧 -
Group 4	one got chilly. Now, isn't that silly?
ALL	So that left 4.
Group 2	Four foolish hippos leap ing on a fence -
Group 4	one hit a and down went he!
ALL	So that left 3.
Group 3	Three tipsy hippos tripping on a 🚧 -
Group 1	one heard a crack and he stepped back!
ALL	So that left 2.
Group 4	Two tired hippos stumbling on a 🚧 -
Group 1	one started to doze, so the story goes,
ALL	so that left 1.
Group 2	1 lonely sitting on a fence.
Group 3	It made no sense being the only one -
ALL	so that left none.

Early Literacy - A Seasonal Approach

My Otter Ideas

Early Literacy - A Seasonal Approach

Activities listed on this page are applicable to stories grouped in particular theme areas. Consider partnering the feature story with one or two others listed from the same category, then use the reproducibles for introductory or follow-up activities.

Great Books for Winter   Activities   Page

Snow Fun

Sadie and the Snowman   *Teaching Activities*   42
Norman's Snowball
Winter Games   *A Frosty Friend* - Mini-book   45
Bruno in the Snow
The Mitten   *Dreaming of Winter* - Readers Theatre Script   47
Grandpa Dan's Toboggan Ride
Bruno in the Snow
Ben's Snow Song
The Bungalo Boys III - Champions of Hockey

Winter Weather

Alfie's Long Winter   *The Storm* - Readers Theatre Script   49
Belle's Journey
Snow   *Winter Storms* - Mini-book   50
The Big Storm
The Jacket I Wear in the Snow

Christmas - The Nativity

A Small Miracle   *Everything Went Wrong* - Readers Theatre Script   52
Away in a Manger
Silent Night
The Angel of Mill Street
The Christmas Candle
The Christmas Miracle of Jonathan Toomey
Wombat Divine

Christmas - All About Santa

The Polar Express   *Do You Have a Minute, Santa?* - Readers Theatre Script   54
7 Sleeps Until Christmas
The Crooked Little Christmas Tree
The Twelve Days of Christmas
The Reindeer Christmas
The Special Gifts

Winter Holidays

Franklin's Valentines   *Friends Forever* - Readers Theatre Script   56
Invitation to Readers Theatre

U-Otter-Read-It © 1999

Early Literacy - A Seasonal Approach

Sadie and the Snowman
by Allen Morgan
Before Reading

Changes

preparing for reading by drawing upon personal experiences

Have you wanted something to last forever? What was it? How did you feel when it didn't ? Why did you want it to last? What did you do? Did your plan work? How long is forever?.
Sometimes things can be preserved to last longer than originally intended. What kinds of methods do you know, that help things last longer?
Answers might be:
- put it in the fridge
- cook it
- dry it
- freeze it
- dip it in wax or metal (bronzing)

Record the children's answers, and refer to them in the next activity.

predicting
assessing
critical thinking

Tell the children they are going to read a story about a little girl who wants one thing in particular, to last longer. Introduce Sadie by suggesting that she wants to save her snowman for the summer. Ask the children what they would do to make a snowman last that long. Again, record their responses, which will be different than those given previously, as they now have a specific focus about what is being preserved. Ask them to select answers from the previous discussion, which apply to this situation, and discard those that are not practical. Allow children the opportunity to elaborate on their ideas.

Sharing Experiences

building on personal experiences establishes a knowledge base, and motivates a personal connection with story character and events

Discuss building snowmen with the children. Some questions you might ask:
- Have you made a snowman?
- What was the snow like?
- How did it feel?
- How did it look?
- How did you get the snow to stick together?
- Did you roll it? Pat it?
- How big was your snowman?
- What did you use for eyes, nose, smile?
- How long did it last?

Ask children to draw a picture of their snowman. Give the snowman a name. Write some descriptive words: *gigantic, huge, awesome, tremendous, friendly, lopsided* ... Children may prefer to have some of their peers offer words to describe their snowman, and choose those they feel best suit their drawing.

building vocabulary in a collaborative and supportive setting

Continuing to Build

While children discuss their winter experiences, write words on individual pocket chart cards. Invite the children to work in groups and sort the words according to the following headings:
- Snow Feels Like
- Snow Looks Like
- I can _____ (*actions in the snow or with the snow*)
- What snow does

focusing on word meaning to develop a vocabulary

categorizing to recognize multiple relationships between words - meaning, patterns, and usage

During Reading

Guided Storyboarding

Read the story to the children, inviting them to draw what they hear. In this activity, do not show the illustrations to the children - rather let them create the pictures in their minds first. Initially, stop the story after every page, allowing time for children to draw what they have heard. This activity may require several readings, so that the children have many opportunities to gather, check and confirm the details for their drawings. Encourage them to refer to their drawings, to *follow* along with every reading. The children will end up with 14 sketches. A good way to accommodate this activity is to provide children with a 2 blank pages, folded into 4 sections. Cut along the top - to make a mini-book of 16 pages. The two extra pages will serve as a front and back cover.

focus listening on details, encouraging imagination and personal interpretation of characters and setting

Invite the children to retell the story to a friend, referring to their storyboards for necessary details.

referring to notes supports successful retelling - and builds good study skills for advanced readers. This type of activity introduces notetaking skills on a basic, elementary level.

Early Literacy - A Seasonal Approach

After Reading

WORD SORTING

Based on the needs of your students, select words from the story to sort into categories. Have the children organize the words according to concepts and features which need to be practiced. For example, categories might focus on
- initial consonant sounds
- initial blends
- word meanings
- syllabication
- rhyme.

building word awareness by focusing on grapho-phonemic, semantic or symtactic cues

The word sort might look like the sample given:

Begin with s	weather	food	2 syllables	1 syllable
snow	cold	carrot	snowman	snow
Sadie	freezing	raisins	blanket	ground
smile	summer	zucchini	raccoon	nose
squirrel	warmer	apple	peanuts	good

page 47, 49

Readers Theatre

Read the scripts, *Dreaming of Winter*, and *The Storm* with the children. Use these scripts to introduce children to other aspects of winters, namely winter games, and dangers of winter weather. Other scripts which work nicely with a winter theme:
- *Blustery Winter Blues* (page 38)
- *Dangerous Contraption* (page 40)

from *Invitation to Readers Theatre, A guidebook for using Readers Theatre to celebrate holidays and special events throughout the year.* by Raczuk and Smith.

The mini-book *A Frosty Friend* connects well with the theme of *Sadie and the Snowman* and serves as a useful early reading experience.

page 45

U-Otter-Read-It © 1999

To accompany *Snow Fun* stories

9

a friend!

1

Take two snowballs big and fat,

U-Otter
Hear Me Read!

I have read this book to:

_____

What would you
name your snowman?

A Frosty Friend

Illustrated by _____

7

Frosty Friend- continued

U-Otter-Read-It © 1999

4

put rocks down
the front –
all in a row.

3

Two apples for eyes
and a carrot nose,

5

Don't forget to make
him grin and in the
end you'll have –

2

add a scarf and pop
on a hat.

To accompany *Snow Fun* stories

Dreaming of Winter
by Marilyn Smith

Chorus	Some day -
	Some crisp winter day,
Solo 1	I'll roar down the hill in my wooden toboggan -
Chorus	dashing, flashing,
Solo 1	as quick as can be.
Chorus	Some day -
	Some bright winter day
Solo 2	I'll lace up my skates and sail 'round the pond -
Chorus	gliding, flowing,
Solo 2	as free as can be.
Chorus	Some day -
	Some mild winter day,
Solo 3	I'll sneak up on my Dad with a snowball in hand -
Chorus	throwing, racing,
Solo 3	as scared as can be!
Chorus	Some day -
	Some cool autumn day,
Solo 4	I'll watch as the sky turns cloudy and gray,
	and snowflakes come -
Chorus	drifting,
	floating
	downward
	to earth.
Soloists	Some day -
Chorus	Some day soon!

The Storm

by Marilyn Smith

Reader 1   Outside, the wind is raging,
           the snow is swirling round.
           Inside, my heart is yearning
           to know you're safe and sound.

Reader 2   Outside, the sun is setting
           and darkness starts to creep.
           Inside my mind, I ponder,
           as worry prevents my sleep.

Reader 3   Against the glass I'm pressing.
           I peer into the night.
           I pace the floor and wonder
           if indeed, you are all right.

Reader 4   May unseen hands direct you -
           leading you homeward bound.
           May peace enfold and calm you -
           'midst loud and frightening sounds.

Reader 1   Soon the door will open,

Reader 3   warm arms will draw you in.

Reader 4   Inside, we'll watch the fire -

Reader 2   safe from the howling wind.

Note: children might enjoy introducing this script by creating a soundscape, using voices to imitate the sounds of raging winds and howling winds. Encourage a build-up of sound, leading in to the script, then end the script with the same sounds.

Early Literacy - A Seasonal Approach

My Otter Ideas

6

_____
_____
_____
_____

and I

U-Otter
Hear Me Read!

I have read this book to:

_____

Name three things people should carry in their cars to be prepared for storms.

U-Otter-Read-It © 1999 May be reproduced for classroom use

7

1

_____
_____
_____
_____

In a big storm,

Winter Storms

Written and Illustrated by

To accompany *Winter Weather* stories

Winter Storms - continued

U-Otter-Read-It © 1999

4

3

The ice

The snow

The people

The wind

5

2

To accompany Nativity stories

Everything Went Wrong
by Marilyn Smith

Reader 1   At the Christmas pageant practice,
           everything went wrong!

Reader 3   The shepherds tripped and dropped their crooks

Reader 2   while Mary sang her song.

Reader 4   The wisemen never did arrive
           'cause they got lost backstage!

Reader 3   Mrs. Jensen played odd notes
           whenever she turned a page.

Reader 1   The halos of the angels
           were rather topsy turvy,

Reader 2   bobbing constantly up and down
           while keeping time superbly.

Reader 4   The donkey from the children's zoo
           brayed in Joseph's face.

Reader 2   The reader got the giggles
           then promptly lost his place.

Reader 3   The curtains wouldn't open

Reader 1   and then they wouldn't close -
           to hide the wobbly scenery
           that threatened to end the show.

Reader 4	In spite of all the problems
Reader 3	regardless of the flaws,
Reader 2	the director smiled calmly
ALL	at everything she saw.
Reader 4	She didn't lose her temper, crying -
Director	"This will never do!"
Reader 3	Instead, she sent us on our way When everything was through.
Reader 1	She said,
Director	"You're already perfect … Perfect in His sight Because He loves us as we are, our play will be
ALL	JUST RIGHT!"
Reader 1	So, maybe things went wrong that day, And perhaps things came undone,
Reader 4	but God knows we told the story, to glorify His Son.

To accompany *Santa* stories

Do You Have a Minute, Santa?
by Marilyn Smith

Reader 1	Do you have a minute, Santa, for a bit of a chat?
Reader 2	We have lots and lots of questions about this and about that.
Reader 3	Do you like wearing red?
Reader 4	Is it time for a change?
Reader 2 ALL	Would you rather wear blue - or would that be too strange?
Reader 4	Do you like eating cookies - wherever you stop?
Reader 2	Would you rather munch popcorn and sip soda pop?
Reader 1	Are you nervous on rooftops?
Reader 3	Do you think you might fall?
Reader 2	Does Mrs. Claus worry?
Reader 4	Do you give her a call?

Reader 2	Does your back start to ache?
Reader 3	Do your fingers get frozen from unloading presents that children have chosen?
Reader 4	Are some chimneys too narrow and dirty inside?
Reader 3	Do you sometimes get stuck - unable to slide?
Reader 2	Do you always make lists? Do you check them all twice?
Reader 1	Do you REALLY know who's naughty or nice?
Reader 4	The questions are endless.
Reader 3	The answers unknown.
Reader 1	So let's talk dear Santa -
Reader 2	PLEASE pick up the phone.

To accompany Winter Holiday *stories*

Friends Forever

by Marilyn Smith

Reader 2	Good friends,
Reader 3	best friends,
Reader 1	there, through thick and thin friends.
Reader 1	Old friends,
Reader 2	new friends,
Reader 4	pat you on the back friends.
Reader 3	Clever friends,
Reader 1	bright friends,
Reader 4	help you when you're stuck friends.
Reader 3	Funny friends,
Reader 2	silly friends,
Reader 4	always make you laugh friends.
Reader 2	Close friends,
Reader 3	kind friends,
Reader 4	listen when you're sad friends.
Reader 1	Chatty friends,
Reader 4	sporty friends,
Reader 3	we can play all day friends.
Reader 2	Special friends,
Reader 1	our friends,
Reader 4	always and forever
ALL	FRIENDS!

Early Literacy - A Seasonal Approach

Activities listed on this page are applicable to stories grouped in particular theme areas. Consider partnering the feature story with one or two others listed from the same category, then use the reproducibles for introductory or follow-up activities.

Great Books for Spring	Activities	Page

In the Garden

Frog and Toad are Friends,	*The Garden - Teaching Activities*	*58*
The Important Book		
Carrot Seed	*Planting the Garden - Readers Theatre Script*	60
The Rose in My Garden		
Jamie O'Rourke and the Big Potato	*Spring Is - Reproducible Pattern Page*	61

Changes in the spring

Amos' Sweater	*Sheepish Barbershop - Readers Theatre Script*	62
What's that Noise?		
Bruno Springs Up		
The Birdfeeder Banquet		

Spring Weather

Mister Got to Go	*Drip, Drop, Rain - Readers Theatre Script*	64
Pigs in the Mud in the Middle of the Rud		
Sheep in a Jeep	*Hoe-down for Spring - Readers Theatre Script*	66
Waters		
Simon Welcomes Spring		

Friends and Family Celebrations

I Love you This Much	*Love Comes - Readers Theatre Script*	65
I Love You the Purplest	*Here's to Mothers - Readers Theatre Script*	68
When Mama Comes Home Tonight		
Are You My Mother?	*My Mom - Mini-book*	69
Love You Forever		
The Runaway Bunny		
Just Me and My Mom		
Just Me and My Dad	*Recipe for a Dad - Readers Theatre Script*	71
The Barnyard Dance		

'The Garden' from Frog and Toad Together

by Arnold Lobel

Before Reading

making predictions based on collection of objects allows children the opportunity to bring personal stories and ideas to the reading experience

Bring in some seed packets, seed catalogues, a gardening trowel, gardening gloves, and a flower pot, and / or other gardening tools and paraphernalia. Tell the children that these are some of the things they will hear about in the story. Ask them what they think the story will be about.

establishing and assessing children's background knowledge

Ask the children if they have ever planted a garden, and if so, invite them to tell what is involved in planting a garden. Invite the children to share their gardening stories. Collect words and ideas from the children as they are talking, either on pocket chart cards, or on chart paper. In the discussion, ask about techniques that are especially important, to helping a garden grow, such as mulching, fertilizing, hoeing, and singing! Before reading, ask the children to listen for all the special things Toad does to encourage the seeds to grow.

During Reading

Read the story, asking the following types of questions throughout the reading.
 • How is frog helping toad? Is he being encouraging? Is he a friend? Why do you think so?
 • How is frog feeling when _____ happens?   What might Toad try next, to help his garden grow?
 • How do you think plants feel about having a song sung to them?

Sing some good 'helping plants to grow' songs. For example:

 • Plant My Garden, Sylvia Wallach, <u>Rhythm, Reading, Rhyme & Rap,</u> Sylvionics, Chicago.
 • Garden Song, by David Mallet, sung by Peter, Paul & Mary on the CD <u>Peter, Paul & Mommy, Too!</u> Warner Brothers Records
 • Here We Go Round the Mulberry Bush, substituting words to fit the gardening theme.

Read the story again, for enjoyment, this time emphasizing different voices and expressions to highlight the different characters and moods. Children may find repetitive section where they can participate.

After Reading

Read *The Important Book*, by Margaret Wise Brown. Using the book as a model, ask the children to list all the things that are important about a garden. For example
- why do we need or want a garden (flowers or vegetable)
- what does a garden need to grow

fiction provides some true information, which is applicable to a real life situation

Keep a list of the children's ideas, adding to the one they used prior to reading the story. Encourage the children to reconsider their original ideas about gardening before the story was read, and ask which of these same jobs and methods Toad used to help his garden grow. Singing might not be one that was selected! Ask children to assess the methods Toad used, and identify the ones they think were the most useful. Also ask about other things that were happening, over which Toad had no control, for example: sunshine, rain, and time to grow! What are their opinions?

critical thinking

Invite the children to use their ideas, for the reproducible classroom book, entitled: *'The Spring Book'*. Their story might be similar to the following:

*The important thing about rain is
that it makes a garden grow.
The important thing about the sun
is that it warms up the soil so the garden can grow.
but the important thing about planting
a garden is that you have to be patient.*

page 61

The classroom book may also be expanded to include other important spring topics such as: earthworms, robins, umbrellas, thunder, and green grass.

Read the script, *Planting the Garden*. After reading, ask the children to identify the interesting things they noticed about the text. For example, did they notice the repetition of initial consonants? They might enjoy trying to change portions of the script, maintaining the pattern of alliteration and repetition. This would be a good activity to do with classroom buddies from an upper elementary class.

page 60

U-Otter-Read-It © 1999

To accompany *Garden* stories

Planting the Garden

by Marilyn Smith and Helen Raczuk

Reader 3	Pick up a packet,
Reader 1	a packet of seeds,
ALL	it's time to plant the garden.
Reader 2	Dig in the dirt.
Reader 4	Don't dawdle about.
ALL	It's time to plant the garden.
Reader 1	Potatoes, and parsley,
Reader 2	pansies, and peas,
ALL	it's time to plant the garden.
Reader 3	Blueberries, broccoli,
Reader 4	beets, and beans,
ALL	it's time to plant the garden.
Reader 2	Celery, carrots,
Reader 3	cabbage, and corn,
ALL	it's time to plant the garden.
Reader 1	Water, and whistle,
Reader 4	weed, and wait,
ALL	at last, we've planted the garden.

To accompany *Garden* stories

The Spring Book

The important thing about _____

_____ is that _____

_____

_____

_____

_____

_____

_____

_____

_____

_____

_____

But the important thing about _____

_____ is that _____

_____

To accompany *Changes in Spring* stories

Sheepish Barbershop

By Marilyn Smith & Helen Raczuk

Reader 3	A sheep strolled into the barbershop
Reader 1	for his annual springtime trim.
Reader 4	"A little off the top",
Reader 1	said he,
Reader 2	with a smile, and a sheepish grin.
Reader 3	"I've never clipped a sheep before but I'm willing to give it a try."
Reader 4	said the barber, eagerly grabbing his shears,
Reader 1	and the wool began to fly.
Reader 2	With a snip and a clip
Reader 1	and a snippity snip,
Reader 4	the wool piled up -
ALL	everywhere!
Reader 3	The poor sheep shook and he tried not to look,
Reader 2	while he squirmed in the barber's chair.
Reader 1	"Ouch!
Reader 4	Oh No!

Sheepish Barbershop - To accompany *Changes in Spring* stories

Reader 3	Slow down!"
Reader 2	cried the sheep, as his fleece flew down to the floor.
Reader 1	"You really must stop! I am leaving this shop!"
Reader 4	And with that, he stormed out the door.
Reader 3	With his head held high and a tear in his eye,
Reader 2	that sheep marched home to his flock.
Reader 4	But when he arrived, to his great surprise
Reader 2	the other sheep didn't look shocked!
Reader 1 Reader 3	'Nice cut," said one.
Reader 4 Reader 2	"Well done!" said another.
Reader 2, 3 & 4	"Who's your barber?"
Reader 1	asked two or three.
Reader 2	So he lined them all up, saying,
Reader 3	"You can get cut and look just as attractive as me."

To accompany *Spring Weather* stories

Drip Drop Rain
by Marilyn Smith

Group 1	Group 2
drip rain	drop rain
pitter patter	**pitter patter**
splat rain	
	clitter clatter
click rain	
	dancing oh so quick rain
puddles in the street rain	
	mucky muddy feet rain
sliding down the spout rain	
	sprinkling all about rain
drip rain	
	drop rain
STOP!	**STOP!**
stop	
	stop
stop	
	stop
stop	stop

To accompany *Family* stories

Love Comes
by Marilyn Smith

Reader 2	Love comes -
Reader 3	in bright smiles,
Reader 1	in twinkling eyes,
Reader 4	in gentle hugs,
Reader 2	in lullabies.

Reader 3	Love comes -
Reader 4	in silly jokes,
Reader 2	in special mail,
Reader 1	in stories shared,
Reader 3	it never fails.

Reader 1	Love comes -
Reader 4	to dry our tears,
Reader 2	to make us strong,
Reader 3	to calm our fears,
Reader 1	when nights are long.

Reader 4	Love comes -
Reader 1	to those who share,
Reader 3	to those who give,
Reader 2	to those who care,
Reader 4	to those who live.

Reader 2	Love comes -
Reader 1	to light the way,
Reader 3	to touch our hearts
Reader 2	in each new day.
ALL	Love comes.

Hoe-down for Spring

by Marilyn Smith

Reader 1   Hang up your overcoat.
　　　　　 The bird is on the wing.
　　　　　 Get your feet a tappin'
　　　　　 for a springtime fling.

Reader 3   Toss off the woolly hat.
　　　　　 Roll up your sleeves.
　　　　　 Slide into your sandals.

ALL   Fiddle-dee-dee

Reader 4   Twitter with the robins.
Reader 3   Squawk with the crows.
Reader 1   Chirp with the bluejays
　　　　　 while the green grass grows.

Reader 4   Prance around the garden.
Reader 2   Twirl in the rain.
Reader 3   Skip down the sidewalk,
　　　　　 again and again.

Hoe-down for Spring - To accompany *Spring Weather* stories

Reader 1	With a hoot and a holler and a
ALL	HULL-A-BA-LOO!

Reader 3	Call to your neighbour, saying -
Reader 2	How do you do?
Reader 4	Bow to the east.
Reader 1	Bow to the west.
Reader 2	Do a little jig and then take a rest.
Reader 3	Do-si-do 'round the poplar tree.
ALL	Then lead all your friends to the springtime jamboree.

To accompany *Family* stories

Here's to Mothers

by Marilyn Smith

Reader 2	Here's to mothers who wash dirty socks,
Reader 3	sweep up dust bunnies,
Reader 1	bandage our knees,
Reader 4	and read us the funnies.
Reader 1	Here's to mothers who drive us to soccer,
Reader 3	drive us to swim,
Reader 4	drive us to piano,
Reader 2	and drive us to gym.
Reader 3	Here's to mothers who plan birthday parties,
Reader 2	cheer at our games,
Reader 1	cry at our plays,
Reader 4	and splash in the rain.
Reader 3	Here's to mothers who cuddle and read,
Reader 4	listen and talk,
Reader 2	tease and laugh,
Reader 1	'right round the clock.
Reader 2	Here's to mothers short and tall,
Reader 4	young and old,
Reader 1	one and all!!
Reader 3	For all that you do,
Reader 2	Here's to
ALL	YOU!

To accompany *Friends and Family* stories

9

_____
_____
_____
_____
_____
_____
_____
_____
_____
_____

My Mom is Special

U-Otter Hear Me Read!
I have read this book to:

My Mom

Written and Illustrated
By _____
Grade _____

My Mom - continued

U-Otter-Read-It © 1999

My Favourite Memory

If I had 3 wishes
for my mom, I'd wish ...

Recipe for a Dad

by Marilyn Smith

Reader 1   Take one man
          with a great big grin,

Reader 4   two arms to cuddle,

Reader 2   and whiskers on his chin.

Reader 3   Give him a child
          to teach and to guide,

Reader 4   Lego™ to build with
          and bicycles to ride.

ALL   Fold in computers,
          or workshops and tools.

Reader 1   Hockey and football
          or hiking is cool.

Reader 2   Stir in some tickles,
          blend in some play,

Reader 4   sprinkle with laughter,

Reader 3   and call it a day!

Early Literacy - A Seasonal Approach

My Otter Ideas

Early Literacy - A Seasonal Approach

Activities listed on this page are applicable to stories grouped in particular theme areas. Consider partnering the feature story with one or two others listed from the same category, then use the reproducibles for introductory or follow-up activities.

Great Books for Summer   Activities   Page

Summer Sports

Take me Out to the Ballgame   Teaching Activities   74
Bats About Baseball   *A Fan's Request* - Readers Theatre Script   76
Albert's Ballgame
Matthew and the Midnight Ballgame

Summer Gardens

Jamberry   *A "Berry" Good Skipping Rhyme* -   77
Blueberries for Sal   Readers Theatre Script
Bruno and the Bees

Creepy, climbing, flying, slithering things

Have You seen Bugs?   *Any Kind of Bugs* - Readers Theatre Script   79
Have you seen Birds?
The Very Hungry Caterpillar
The Grouchy Ladybug
The Sparrow's Song
I Went Walking

U-Otter-Read-It © 1999

Take Me Out To The Ballgame
by MaryAnn Kovalski

Before Reading

assessing prior knowledge, vocabulary

Tell the children the title of the story that will be read. Ask them to predict the content of the story, based on the title alone. Which 'ballgame' do children think the story will be about?

Invite the children to share stories of baseball experiences - either as a player, or a spectator. Note the vocabulary used and list baseball terminology used. Gather words such as: *base, catcher, homeplate, loaded, homerun, mitt, glove, curve ball, stadium, bat, pop fly, inning, walk, umpire,* etc., on a chart or set of pocket chart cards.

During Reading

Baseball Trivia - this favourite summertime game was developed in the early 1800's as a variation of the English sport: Cricket. Today, Americans claim baseball as their national sport. Unlike other sports that have a time limit on them, baseball isn't over until the last runner is out, thus the famous quote by Yogi Berra: 'It's not over 'till it's over.'

Mary Ann's book is based on an originial song, which became a favourite and remains popular today. It is sung with great enthusiasm during baseball season. Children may enjoy learning the song so they can sing along during the reading. Another delightful and humorous song is Right Field by Willy Welch. It can be found on the CD by Peter, Paul and Mary entitled <u>Peter, Paul, and Mommy, Too!</u> , Warner Brothers Records.

Invite children to identify baseball terms in the song, and in the script. *Flyball, pitcher* - are words which may require additional explanation.

After Reading

Children may enjoy researching famous baseball personalities, or learning the rules for the game and playing - if they have not already had the opportunity to do so. Children might also enjoy writing their own set of rules for the game of baseball - as they understand it. Guide their writing by asking questions such as:

- How many runners can there be at any time?
- What is a home run?
- What does it mean to be out?
- What is a foul ball?
- Why does the pitcher stand on a mound?
- What is a base?
- Who are all the players on a team? What are their jobs?

Use the word cards or chart of words, to assist children while writing. Some might like to keep a collection of words in a personal 'word book' to use as reference for future reference. Encourage those children to add definitions or drawings to help them remember more about the words.

Play baseball! Use the children's rules, and then teach them the proper rules. This might provide an interesting opportunity to discuss the importance of rules in a team sport, and the concept of being a 'team player'.

Older children may enjoy hearing or reading the poem: *Casey at the Bat,* by Ernest Lawrence Thayer. This poem has also been scripted for readers theatre, and can be found in *Readers Theatre Scripted Rhymes and Rhythms,* by Carl Braun.

Invite children to suggest words about the sensory aspect of baseball. For example:
- baseball sounds like
- looks like
- smells like
- feels like
- tastes like

Collect these words on chart paper, word cards, or some format that can be accessed again easily at a later date, if necessary. Sort the words according to the categories given.

listing descriptive words serves to support student writing and expand vocabulary

Words such as: *crack, slap, slide, whoosh, smack, oomph, yeah, roar, hooray* - may be offered as the *sounds* of baseball. Using the following pattern, create a 'chain' of words about baseball.

             line 1 - *name of the game*
                line 2 - *sights*
               line 3 - *sounds*
           line 4 - *actions / verbs*
               line 5 - *sounds*
                line 6 - *sights*
line 7 - *another name for the game*

providing children with a format or pattern supports reluctant or insecure writers

To accompany *Summer Sports* stories

A Fan's Request

By Marilyn Smith

Reader 3	Give me a chance to go to the game,
Reader 1	on sunny days, cold days, or even in *rain*.
Reader 4	Give me the thrill, the **roar** of the crowd,
Reader 2	the crack of the bat as we look to the clouds.
Reader 3	Give me the drinks and hot dog buns,
Reader 4	while we cheer for the home team to score a few runs.
Reader 1	Give me a glove - my old one is fine,
Reader 2	in case a FLY ball crosses the line!
Reader 1	Give me a spot that has a good view
Reader 4	of pitchers and batters, and curve balls, too!
Reader 3	Please give an ear to these simple requests.
Reader 2 ALL	If you want to go, please come as my guest!

76

U-Otter-Read-It © 1999
may be copied for classroom use only

A "Berry" Good Skipping Rhyme

by Marilyn Smith

Reader 4	One berry, two berry,
Reader 2	three berry, four.
Reader 3	Pick a pail of berries or
Reader 1	buy them at the store.
Reader 3	Blueberry, blackberry,
Reader 4	raspberry, pie.
Reader 2	Skip to the beat now -
Reader 1	my, oh my!
Reader 3	Strawberry, chokecherry,
Reader 4	brambleberry, jam.
Reader 1	Hop on one foot,
Reader 2	as fast as you can.
Reader 4	Cranberry, gooseberry,
Reader 1	boysenberry cake.
Reader 2	Jump up and down
Reader 3	to stay awake!
Reader 1	Red berries,
Reader 4	purple berries,
Reader 2	tasty treats!
ALL	How many berries can YOU eat?

To accompany *Creepy, Crawly* stories

Any Kind of Bugs
by Marilyn Smith and Helen Raczuk

ALL	We like bugs.
Reader 1	Any kind of bugs.
Reader 2	Striped bugs.
Reader 3	Speckled bugs.
Reader 4	Shiny bugs.
Reader 2	Darting
Reader 1	Leaping
Reader 3	Gliding
Reader 4	Whirling
ALL	We like bugs.
Reader 3	A bug on the ceiling
Reader 4	A bug in a thicket
Reader 1	A bug on a leaf
Reader 2	A bug in the air
Reader 4	Batches of butterflies
Reader 3	Bunches of beetles
Reader 2	Billions of bees
ALL	Beautiful bugs

Early Literacy - A Seasonal Approach

My Otter Ideas

Early Literacy - A Seasonal Approach

Title	Author	Publisher	ISBN
7 Sleeps Until Christmas	Adams, Stuart	Stuart Adams Communications	0968396305
A-Z	Boynton, Sandra	Little Simon, New York	0671493175
A Mountain Alphabet	Ruurs, Margriet	Toronto: Tundra Books	088776374X
A Small Miracle	Collington, Peter	Alfred A. Knopf	0679887253
Albert's Ballgame	Tryon, Leslie	Aladdin Paperbacks (Simon & Schuster)	0689823495
Alfie's Long Winter	McEvoy, Greg	Stoddart Kids, Toronto	0773729100
Amos' Sweater	Lunn, Janet	Groundwood Books	088899074X
Angel of Mill Street, The	Weller, Frances Ward	Philomel Books	0399231331
Animal Rap and Far Out Fables	Molnar, Gwen	Beach Holme Publishing	08878368X
Are You My Mother?	Eastman, PD	Random House, Canada	0679890475
Auction, The	Andrews, Jan	Meadow Mouse Paperback	0888991681
Away in a Manger	Hayes, Sarah	Overlea House	0 717221687
Bats About Baseball	Little, Jean	Penguin, Toronto	0670852708
Barnyard Dance	Boynton, Sandra	Workman Publishing, N.Y	1563054426
Belle's Journey	Reynolds, Marilynn	Orca Books	1551430215
Ben's Snow Song	Hutchins, Hazel	Annick Press, Toronto	0920303900
Bibi and the Bull·	Vaage, Carol	Dragon Hill, Edmonton	1896124003
Big Storm, The	Tregebov, Rhea	Kids Can Press	1550741179
Birdfeeder Banquet	Martchenko, Michael	Annick Press, Toronto	1550371460
Blueberries for Sal	McCloskey, Robert	Penguin, Canada	0670175919
Brenda and Edward	Kovalski, Maryann	Kids Can Press	1550741403
Brown Bear, Brown, Bear, What Do You See?	Martin, Bill Jr.	Henry Holt & Co.	0805002014
Bruno and the Bees	Daigneault, Sylvie	Harper Collins, Toronto	0006481450
Bruno in the Snow	Daigneault, Sylvie	Harper Collins, Toronto	0006479537
Bruno Springs Up	Daigneault, Sylvie	Harper Collins, Toronto	0006418248
Bungalo Boys III - Champions of Hockey, The	Bianchi, John	Bungaloo Books, Canada	0921285167
Carrot Seed, The	Kraus, Ruth	Scholastic	0590003860
Christmas Candle, The	Evans, Richard Paul	Simon & Schuster	0689823193
Christmas Miracle of Jonathan Toomey, The	Wojciechowski, Susan	Candlewick Press, Massachusetts	1564023206
Crooked Little Christmas Tree, The	Cutting, Michael	Scholastic, Canada	0590736523
Doggies	Boynton, Sandra	Little Simon, NY	0671493183
Eenie Meenie Manitoba	Heidbreder, Robert	Kids Can Press, Toronto	1550743015
First Red Maple Leaf ,The	Zeman, Ludmila	Tundra Books, Toronto	0887763723
Four Seasons for Toby	Harris, Dorothy Joan	Scholastic-Tab, Canada	059071676X
Franklin Goes to School	Bourgeois, Paulette	Kids Can Press	1555074268X
Franklin's Blanket	Bourgeois, Paulette	Kids Can Press	1550742787

Early Literacy - A Seasonal Approach

• Franklin's Halloween	Bourgeois, Paulette	Kids Can Press	1550742833
• Franklin's Valentine	Bourgeois, Paulette	Cartwheel Books	0590130013
• Frog and Toad Together	Lobel, Arnold	Harper Trophy	006440214
• Grandpa Dan's Toboggan Ride	Reid, Suzan	Scholastic, Canada	0590740601
• Guess How Much I Love You	McBratney, Sam	Candlewick Press	1564024733
• Have You Seen Birds	Oppenheim, Joanne	Scholastic, Canada	0590715771
• Have You Seen Bugs?	Oppenheim, Joanne	Scholastic, Canada	059012496X
• How Santa Got His Job	Krensky, Stephen	Simon and Schuster	0689806973
• I Love You the Purplest	Joosse, Barbara M.	Chronicle Books	0811807185
• I Went Walking	Williams, Sue	Voyager Books, New York	0152380116
• Important Book, The	Brown, Margaret Wise	Harper Collins	0060207205
• Invitation to Munsch	Raczuk & Smith	U-Otter-Read-It	0968107400
• Invitation to Readers Theatre, celebrating holidays	Raczuk & Smith	U-Otter-Read-It	0968107419
• Ira Sleeps Over	Waber, Bernard	Houghton Mifflin	0395205034
• It's the First Day of School	Schultz, Charles M.	Harper Festival	0694009113
• Jacket I Wear in the Snow, The	Neitzel, Shirley	Mulberry Books, New York	0688080286
• Jamie O'Rourke and the Big Potato	DePaola, Tomie	Putnam & Grosset	0698116038
• Jamberry	Degen, Bruce	Harper Collins	0060214163
• Jillian Jiggs to the Rescue	Gilman, Phoebe	Scholastic	0590241788
• Just Me and My Dad	Mayer, Mercer	Golden Book New York	0307118398
• Just Me and My Mom	Mayer, Mercer	Golden Book New York	030712584X
• Love You Forever	Munsch, Robert	Firefly Books, Toronto	0920668372
• Mama's Bed	Bogart, Jo Ellen	Scholastic, Toronto	0590743120
• Matthew And The Midnight Ball Game	Morgan, Allen	Toronto: Stoddart Kids	0773758534
• Mister Got To Go	Simmie, Lois	Red Deer College Press	0889951276
• Mitten, The	Brett, Jan	G.P. Putnam's Sons, N.Y.	039921920X
• Mouse Paint	Walsh, Ellen Stoll	Harcourt Brace Children's Books	0152002650
• My Arctic 123	Kusugak, Michael	Annick Press, Toronto	1550375040
• My Crayons Talk	Hubbard, Patricia	Henry Holt and Co., New York	0805061509
• My Little Sister Ate One Hare	Grossman, Bill	Dragonfly Books, New York	051788576X
• My Love For You	Roth, Susan L.	Dial Books	0802755523520
• Norman's Snowball	Hutchins, Hazel	Annick Press, Toronto	1550370502
• November Boots	Hundal, Nancy	Harper Collins, Toronto	0006480772
• Oliver Pig At School	Van Leeuwen, Jean	Puffin Books	0140371451
• One Grey Mouse	Burton, Katherine	Kids Can Press	1550742256
• Pigs in the Mud in the Middle of the Rud	Plourde, Lynn	Blue Sky Press (Scholastic)	0590568639
• Polar Express, The	Van Allsburg, Chris	Houghton Mifflin	0395389496

• **Puddles**	London, Jonathan	Puffin Books	0670872180
• **Pumpkin Blanket, The**	Zagwyn, Deborah Turney	Fitzhenry and Whiteside	1550410970
• **Quilt Story, The**	Johnston, Tony	Penguin Putnam Books	0698113683
• **Readers Theatre Scripted Rhymed and Rhythms**	Braun, Carl & Win	Braun and Braun Educational	1895805309
• **Red is Best**	Stinson, Kathy	Annick Press	092023626X
• **Reindeer Christmas, The**	Price, Moe	Doubleday, Canada	0385255470
• **Rose in My Garden, The**	Lobel, Arnold	Scholastic	0590335847
• **Runaway Bunny, The**	Brown, Margaret Wise	Harper & Row Publishers	0064430189
• **Sadie and the Snowman**	Morgan, Allen	Kids Can Press	0919964788
• **Selina and the Bear Paw Quilt**	Smucker, Barbara	Stoddart	0773758372
• **Sheep in a Jeep**	Shaw, Nancy	Houghton Mifflin	0395470307
• **Sheep in a Shop**	Shaw, Nancy	Houghton Mifflin	0395872766
• **Simon and the Wind**	Tibo, Gilles	Tundra Books	088776276X
• **Simon Welcomes Spring**	Tibo, Gilles	Tundra Books	0887762786
• **Silent Night**	Jeffers, Susan	E.P. Dutton, New York	0525441441
• **Snow**	Shulevitz, Uri	Farrar Straus & Giroux	0374370923
• **Something From Nothing**	Gilman, Phoebe	Scholastic	0590745573
• **Sparrow's Song, The**	Wallace, Ian	Penguin Books, Canada	0670814539
• **Special Gifts, The**	Grosz, Peter	North-South-Books	1558589619
• **Ten Little Rabbits**	Grossman, Virginia	Chronicle Books	0811821323
• **Those Green Things**	Stinson, Kathy		1550373765
• **Toy-Maker, The**	Evans, Denise	Scholastic, Toronto	0590716832
• **Trick or Treat, Little Critter**	Mayer, Mercer	Golden Book New York	0307127915
• **Turtle Spring**	Zagwyn, Deborah Turney	Tricycle Press, Berkeley	1883672538
• **Twelve Days of Christmas, The**	Brett, Jan	G.P. Putnam's Sons	0399221972
• **Very Hungry Caterpillar, The**	Carle, Eric	Putnam Publishing	0399213015
• **Grouchy Ladybug, The**	Carle, Eric	Harper Collins, Canada	0060270888
• **Waters**	Chase, Edith Newlin	Scholastic, Canada	0590742019
• **What's That Noise?**	Lemieux, Michele	Kids Can Press	0921103697
• **Wheels**	Hughes, Shirley	Douglas & McIntyre, Ltd.	0888948379
• **Wheels on the Bus, The**	Kovalski, Maryann	Kids Can Press	0921103921
• **When Mama Comes Home Tonight**	Spinelli, Eileen	Simon and Schuster	0689810652
• **Whispering Cloth, The**	Shea, Pegi Deitz	Boyds Mill Press	1563971348
• **Wildlife 1,2,3, Counting Book, The**	Thornhill, Jan	Owl Greey de Pencier Books	1895688140
• **Winter Games**	Pare, Roger	Annick Press, Toronto	1550371843
• **Wombat Divine**	Fox, Mem	Harcourt Brace	0142014160

U-Otter-Read-It
11 Miller Place, Spruce Grove, Alberta, Canada T7X 2N1
Phone: (780) 962-9854 • Fax: (780) 962-9854
Email: olannaz@istar.ca or check our web site: http://www.uotter.com

U-Otter-Read-It Seminars and Workshops

Helen and Marilyn are happy to design workshops specific to the needs of your PD organization or conference. Call today, to discuss options. U-Otter-Read-It Phone or fax: (780) 962 9854

Invitation to Readers Theatre
Looking for an interesting and fun way to get children reading? Readers theatre reinforces literacy skills in a supportive and creative manner. A wide range of original scripts, based on favourite stories and themes will be read and developed in this interactive seminar.
Content focus - primary
Time - 90 min. minimum

An Otter Invitation to Readers Theatre
Participants will work through scripts based on folktales, legends and stories from cultures around the world. Activities will be shared for connecting to social studies, language arts and other curriculum areas, as well as introducing and expanding issues relating to personal understanding of self and others.
Content focus - upper elementary, junior high
Time - 90 min. minimum

Teachers and Parents - working together
Worried about what to say at 'meet the teacher night'? Do you freeze when faced with questions such as:
• How is my child doing?
• What does this mean on the report card?
• How can I help my child at home?
• What kind of a reading program is this anyway? This session is designed to provide teachers with the tools needed to address issues and concerns parents have with reading instruction in the classroom. Reproducible handouts to share with parents, along with record keeping / sharing ideas, reproducible overhead presentations, and guidelines for a parent-teacher presentation will be provided.
Content focus - primary
Time - 90 min. minimum

Early Literacy - strategies, stories and scripts
There are a variety of techniques teachers can use which are essential to developing a good early childhood program. Learn how to guide students to become motivated and independent readers by establishing self-sustaining strategies. Readers theatre, pocket charting, running records, student profiles are some of the topics which will be explored in this practical hands-on session.
Content focus - primary
Time - 90 min. minimum

" WOW! Thanks so much. I teach FSL grade 7 - 9, and there are MANY ideas here …. I'm looking forward to putting them to use.'… Julia Drefs, High Prairie, Alberta "

" 'It was so good, it was like taking a bite of a cookie and wanting more.' … D. Stefishen, Sherwood Park, Alberta "

" As an education student, this workshop gave me encouragement and made me eager to attempt some of the techniques mentioned …. Renee Germain, Medicine Hat, Alberta "

Parents and Literacy Sessions
(PALS)Concerned about what you can do to help your child be ready for school? Find that making choices about books, and pre-writing activities overwhelming? This session will explore picture books, pre-school games and activities designed to guide children easily into first grade. **Content** focus - primary
Time - 90 min. minimum

" Great! Even as someone, who has used Readers Theatre for several years in Jr. high drama, I gained new insights and ideas I can take back and use immediately. ' … J Kryzanowski, St. Albert, Alberta "

" What a thrilling re-awakening to the many creative aspects of encouraging children to appreciate literature! I can't wait to try your intriguing ideas with my class… L. Benn, Medicine Hat "

Check our web site **www.uotter.com** for updates regarding a session in your area, or more information for seminars and sessions available for your staff or association.

U-Otter-Read-It © 1999

U-Otter-Read-It

11 Miller Place, Spruce Grove, Alberta, Canada T7X 2N1
Phone: (780) 962-9854 • Fax: (780) 962-9854
Email: olannaz@istar.ca or check our web site: http://www.uotter.com

Order Form

SHIP TO:
Company/School _____
Address _____
City, Province _____
Postal Code _____
Fax: _____ Phone: _____

Ordered by _____
Authorized by _____

BILL TO:
Company/School _____
Address _____
City, Province _____
Postal Code _____
Contact Person _____

U-Otter-Read-It Ordering Policy*
* As of July 1, 1999, orders under $100 must be accompanied by full payment. Over $100, include 50% of order total. Call, if other arrangements are required.
* No returns will be accepted without prior authorization.
* Call for special group order rates

PAYMENT BY:

Check ☐ Amt. Enclosed _____
Money Order Amt. Enclosed _____
Date Ordered _____

Purchase Order Number: _____
Ship Via: _____

ITEM NO.	DESCRIPTION	Retail	QTY.	TOTAL
001 - MTG	Invitation to Munsch, Vol. I ISBN 0-9681074-0-0	$22.95		
002 - RTG	Invitation to Readers Theatre Celebrating Holidays & Special Events Throughout the Year ISBN 0-9681074-1-9	$22.95		
003 - RTG2	Invitation to Readers Theatre - Book 2 Celebrating Stories of Our Canadian Heritage ISBN 0-9681074-2-7	$22.95		
004 - ELS	Early Literacy: A Seasonal Approach ISBN 0-9681074-3-5	$22.95 NEW		
005 - VRT	A Vocal Invitation to Readers Theatre ISBN 0-9681074-4-3	TBA NEW		
OTP - 1	Otter Teacher Package 1 • Invitation to Readers Theatre • Animal Rap & Far Out Fables by Gwen Molnar	$28.95		
OTP - 2	Otter Teacher Package 2 • Invitation to Readers Theatre (002 -RTG) • Invitation to Readers Theatre - Book 2 (003-RTG2)	$41.95		
001 - MOT	Invitation to Munsch, Overhead Transparencies, set of 5	$8.00		
RT - 30-9	Readers Theatre, Scripted Rhymes & Rhythms Braun & Braun ISBN 1-895805-30-9	$19.95		
RT - 32-5	Readers Theatre, More Scripted Rhymes & Rhythms Braun & Braun ISBN 1-895805-32-5	$19.95		
RTYC-36-8	Readers Theatre for Young Children Braun & Braun ISBN 1-895805-36-8	$23.95		

Shipping and Handling Charges:
up to $30.00   add $3.00
$31.00 to $50.00   add $4.50
$51.00 to $100.00   add 8%
$101.00 to $500.00 add 7%
over $500.00   add 5%

Gst #894 121 599

Subtotal _____
Shipping _____
GST 7% _____
Grand Total _____

Prices subject to change without notice. Please make cheques payable to: U-Otter-Read-It

☐ I would like to be added to your mailing list
☐ Please send information for Professional Development Sessions

U-Otter-Read-It © 1999